Urban Growth and Land Development

The Land Conversion Process

NATIONAL ACADEMY OF SCIENCES | NATIONAL ACADEMY OF ENGINEERING

ADVISORY COMMITTEE TO THE DEPARTMENT OF HOUSING AND URBAN DEVELOPMENT

The report of the Subcommittee was reviewed and approved by the main committee:

Urban Growth and Land Development:
The Land Conversion Process

URBAN GROWTH

AND

LAND DEVELOPMENT

The Land Conversion Process

Report of the
LAND USE SUBCOMMITTEE
of the
ADVISORY COMMITTEE TO THE
DEPARTMENT OF HOUSING
AND URBAN DEVELOPMENT

NATIONAL ACADEMY OF SCIENCES
NATIONAL ACADEMY OF ENGINEERING
WASHINGTON, D.C. 1972

Available from

Printing and Publishing Office
National Academy of Sciences
2101 Constitution Avenue
Washington, D.C. 20418

ISBN 0-309-02044-1
Library of Congress Catalog Card Number 72-86800

Printed in the United States of America

PREFACE

In April 1971, the Land Use Subcommittee of the NAS-NAE Advisory Committee to the Department of Housing and Urban Development (ACHUD), under the chairmanship of Robert C. Wood, was founded to examine the complex relations that exist between the way land is developed and the problems resulting from urbanization.

The Subcommittee's mandate was open-ended. It generated from a commonly held perception that America's rapid urban growth had not been accompanied by a similar growth in the quality of urban life. Many have viewed the process associated with the development and use of land as one of the primary reasons for the divergence between data reflecting urbanization and data descriptive of a "decent living environment."

This report clearly reflects the Subcommittee's decision to grant primacy to an analysis of the land conversion process and to its effect on urban growth problems. Apart from the mandate given by the parent Committee and the resource constraints, study priorities were dictated by the fact that, despite growing public concern, we know relatively little about the import or impact of processes leading either to the development and use of raw land, or to the changes in density and use of developed land. Similarly, and unfortunately, we do not yet understand the effect of the conversion process on land costs or the relationship between such costs and many visible urban growth problems.

The Subcommittee began its efforts by looking back at some of its predecessor committees. An analysis of their studies is contained in Chapter 1 of this report. Briefly, this analysis describes the consensus that apparently developed during the 1960's and early 1970's concerning urban growth and land development problems and the solutions to these problems. Despite this consensus, however, the nation still appears far from developing appropriate policies and programs to meet the challenges caused by continued urbanization. In retrospect, it seems that many past assumptions were in error, particularly those related to population growth, which guided those looking at urban growth and related land development problems in the 1960's and early 1970's. Chapter 2 comments on a number of these assumptions and then briefly states the collective judgment of the Subcommittee concerning a realistic set of assumptions for present and future policy-makers.

Chapter 3 presents a general analysis of the land conversion process and the impact of this process on select urban growth issues. Of particular importance here are the Committee's findings concerning the effect of the conversion process on land costs and the ultimate cost of housing. Finally, Chapter 4 outlines several criteria that the Subcommittee feels should govern the allocation of federal funds for urban growth and land conversion purposes. This chapter also proposes several research and demonstration projects for immediate federal funding. If carried out, these projects will go a long way toward providing the analytical base and empirical evidence necessary for development of more effective urban strategies. In effect, only if government officials gain access to more information than now exists relevant to land, and only if they premise their actions on more realistic assumptions than heretofore, will they be able to define realistic and comprehensive urban growth policies and programs.

The Subcommittee has, throughout this report, called attention to many of the key data gaps concerning processes associated with the development, use, and perhaps abuse of urban land. Similarly, it has, where appropriate, seen fit to challenge many of the all too easily accepted conventional wisdoms concerning the land conversion process and its impact.

The Subcommittee wishes to thank several members of the Academy's staff, among them John Laurmann and Cynthia Taeuber, for assisting effectively in its work.

LAND USE SUBCOMMITTEE

CONTENTS

SUMMARY OF FINDINGS
AND RECOMMENDATIONS

LEGACY OF THE PAST

Since 1960, many public and private groups have tried to define a national urban growth policy, particularly as this policy would affect land development in the nation's urban metropolitan areas. The content of their reports is remarkably similar. Most project a high rate of population growth through 2000. All suggest that *without public intervention* the quality of the American environment, and subsequently the quality of American life, will deteriorate rapidly. Most, however, view the public's capacity to mount successful programs to meet urban growth problems as marginal.

Generally the task forces found it easier to sketch out a range of sometimes consistent, sometimes inconsistent, programs than to define a set of coordinated growth and land development policies. Words like "balanced" or "rational" growth simultaneously seem to reflect a desire to set land use objectives and an inability to achieve consensus relative to what these objectives ought to be.

A REALISTIC SET OF ASSUMPTIONS

Apart from developing a consensus that something needs to be done, the nation has not made much progress toward developing a national urban growth and land development policy. One of the key reasons for this is the failure to develop a set of realistic assumptions concerning population growth, distribution, and land consumption.

Considerations related to a national urban growth and land development policy should anticipate a population that, based on current trends, will be far less than that projected in the mid-1960's, concerned primarily with population growth and distribution in metropolitan areas, and focused primarily on differential growth patterns occurring in central city and suburban areas.

THE CONVERSION PROCESS

Given the popularity of the subject among government officials, urban analysts, and laymen alike, we know surprisingly little about how the land conversion process functions or its real impact. What little we do know suggests that much of the conventional wisdom about the effect of the conversion process on land prices must be re-examined prior to creation of national policy or programs. For example, the "problem" of excessively rising land prices in most metropolitan areas seems limited to select growth areas and acreage within growth areas. Clearly, the owners of vacant land as a group are not making untoward profits; second, raw land rarely exceeds 15 percent of total housing costs and, in most instances, ranges only between 2 and 10 percent of the total cost of a unit. Site development costs appear in some areas to be rising faster than land costs and, in absolute dollars, are often far more important than raw land costs.

Although land costs may not be, from a policy and program point of view, the key problem associated with efforts to reduce housing costs, often such costs and the conversion process leading to them have served to ration land for different uses. For example, (a) the absence of land use policies and guidelines from state or metropolitan governments relegates the primary public role in the conversion process to often-competing local governments. Their actions as reflected in zoning, tax, and assessment practices affect the allocation and distribution of land uses. (b) The rapid opening of relatively less expensive land in suburban and fringe areas has had a negative effect on the capital value of land and buildings closer to the central city.

(c) Misinformation about the land market has led to decisions to hold in open space land that is ripe for development. This has increased pressure on land in the path of urban growth and has apparently skewed land development patterns. (d) Because builders convert land prices into housing costs, even nominal increases in raw land costs may deny the use of suburban or fringe land to lower-income families.

ALLOCATION CRITERIA, SELECTED DEMONSTRATIONS, AND NEEDED RESEARCH

This Subcommittee is hesitant to recommend a comprehensive national urban growth policy based primarily on the problems of land development. What we do know about land development problems suggests that, while important, they are not yet crucial. Further, even if we knew more, we doubt that it would be possible to define a meaningful growth policy, given the heterogenic character of the nation's population and the resultant pluralism of its institutions.

The Subcommittee is convinced, however, that there is enough evidence to develop firm criteria for the allocation of federal funds. It is also convinced that the federal government should immediately initiate several demonstrations aimed at building up the capacity of state and metropolitan jurisdictions to successfully influence the land conversion process and a policy and program of research directed at providing a better understanding of the land conversion process.

CRITERIA

Clear priority should be granted in the allocation and distribution of federal funds to (a) those state and metropolitan areas that have prepared or are in the process of preparing areawide development plans; (b) those local projects that are consistent with state and metropolitan plans or planning processes; (c) those housing and community development projects that are larger in scale than predefined state and/or metropolitan minimum requirements; (d) those state and metropolitan areas that have included in their plans meaningful housing strategies to increase housing opportunities in suburban and fringe areas for low- and moderate-income households; and (e) those projects that respond to the needs of low- and moderate-income households.

DEMONSTRATIONS

We propose that the federal government design and initiate a number of demonstrations in a carefully selected group of state and metropolitan areas. These demonstration programs would include use of the following: (a) a single management and planning grant and a possible single point of entry for all federal funds concerned with land and community development; (b) a range of incentives to increase housing options for low- and moderate-income households in suburban and fringe areas; (c) several types of land banks; (d) varying types of extraterritorial land acquisition processes; (e) alternate strategies to dispose of federal land; (f) various strategies to recoup provisions in the disposal of public land; and (g) the New Communities Program to test predefined state and metropolitan objectives concerning land development.

RESEARCH

We propose that the federal government fund several essential research projects. These projects would include development of (a) a raw land price index; (b) single definitions of commonly used terms concerning land conversion; (c) a firmer understanding of the participants in the land conversion process and the effect of their participation; (d) a more precise understanding of the factors affecting the price of land and their relations to one another; (e) a better understanding of how the present array of federal, state, and local taxes affect land conversion and land prices; and (f) a better understanding of current assessment practices and possible alternatives, including the benefits and costs of federal involvement.

CHAPTER ONE

LEGACY OF THE PAST

Since 1960, several White House task forces, countless congressional committees, and many public interest groups have attempted to define the outlines of a national urban growth policy, particularly as this policy affects the conversion of land from rural to urban areas. They have taken as their starting point the widespread conviction that "urban growth does not take place the way it should."[1]

Even though these committees and task forces span a decade and three administrations, their respective products are remarkably similar in coverage, major themes, and proposals.[2] Most begin by projecting the nation's population growth, generally to either 1985 or the year 2000. All accepted the highest estimates of the Bureau of Census demographers, who anticipate a net increase of anywhere from 80 million to 145 million Americans by the turn of the century.

According to almost all groups, without public intervention, most new citizens will inherit steadily growing, already overcrowded, and poorly planned metropolitan areas. Their neighbors will include many newly arrived in-migrants from rural areas and small urban places. Far too many Americans will remain residents of substandard housing located in central cities.

These reports frequently project visions of an emerging problem-laden urban society. In successive and often dramatically juxtaposed picture frames, they portray urban America in the year 2000 as metropolises that are split along color lines, with most blacks in decaying older cities and whites in nearby suburbs; monumentally ugly; wasteful and destructive of natural and human resources; "scandals" of air and water pollution; daily overburdened with ever increasing traffic congestion; plagued by a crazy quilt pattern of inept governmental jurisdictions; and provided with public services, the quantity and quality of which relate not to need but to the fiscal bases of competing general and special purpose governments.

According to most groups, it will be difficult to prevent the projected problems associated with future urbanization: The absence of federal growth and land development policies and programs have denied the federal government leverage in narrowing the distance between a rational measured and balanced urban growth pattern and the anticipated bleak scenario. State governments have been at best marginal and at worst irrelevant in meeting urban and land development problems. Outdated institutions—complemented by lack of interest on the part of state officials—will make the battle to secure more effective state involvement a long one. Even reapportionment may not necessarily assure an improved response to defined growth problems; state legislatures will simply witness a shift from rural to suburban dominance.

Special and general purpose governments in most metropolitan areas have been unable to work together on other than a limited number of common growth or land development problems. Their sheer number, along with the growing diversity of the metropolitan population and scarce revenue sources, will limit their future ability to mount coordinated urban growth strategies. Similarly, most city governments are incapable of successfully influencing, let alone controlling, the urban growth and land development process affecting the well-being of residents living within their political boundaries. Caught between an expanding need for services and a declining fiscal base, general purpose local governments may not be able to contribute much in the future to a national effort to redirect, influence, and control the urban growth process.

Because of their basically similar analyses of urban growth problems, most task forces have presented similar sets of objectives and proposals. Most differences that appear are of degree, not of kind, and generally relate more to the frame of reference or mandate of the group than to competing convictions concerning the appropriateness of alternate objectives and programs.

Task forces have been more adept at sketching a range of programs than in stating national policies about the relationship between urban growth and land development. No task force has prescribed policy goals for population distribution among regional or metropolitan areas. Perhaps as important, none has presented guidelines capable of being translated into public programs for the distribution of specific income or ethnic groups among regional and metropolitan areas. Finally, none has defined objectives for the specific use of land or the linkages among different uses of land in regional or metropolitan areas. Use of undefined terms or phrases like "balanced" or "rational" growth seemingly reflect both a desire to set land use objectives and an inability to achieve consensus about what those objectives should be.

Concerned with institution building at one or more levels of government, more than one task force has proposed the creation of new, or the amendment of existing, institutions at the national level. Some, for example, call for the White House to assume a more active role in setting urban growth and land development policies. One suggested the need for a federal council for development standards; several sought the strengthening of HUD's capacity to deal with urban growth and land conversion problems. A number proposed the need for a co-ordinating mechanism to orchestrate the diverse interests and roles of varied federal agencies.

Although regional institution building received attention from only a few groups who generally sought creation of multistate economic and/or physical planning bodies, almost all task force reports recommended the creation of new or the amendment of existing public agencies at the state, metropolitan, and local levels to meet the problems of urban growth and land conversion. Functions assigned to these agencies ranged from land use planning to actual land acquisition and development.

Generally, task forces have been prone to suggest changes in existing ground rules associated with land development processes. Most would link federal aid for urban and metropolitan growth problems to the development and federal approval of state and/or metropolitan plans; remove remaining federally imposed "workable program" requirements as prerequisites for use of federal programs related to housing or community development; favor the placement of strategic land use control responsibilities in a metropolitan body or the development of a process whereby metropolitan-wide considerations influence local regulation of land use; support revisions in the capital gains tax to provide for a proportionately larger tax on land than on other capital gains; and encourage a reanalysis of local taxing policies and programs to lessen reliance on the property tax.

Those that were more venturesome proposed specific federal, state, or metropolitan preemption of exclusionary local zoning and subdivision ordinances. Many clearly sought a tough reappraisal of overall federal tax laws affecting land development, particularly those provisions that either had the effect of eliminating the putative effects of the capital gains tax, or those that induced land owners—*qua* speculators—to seek shifts in assessed value from land to buildings because of the possibility of rapid depreciation.

Proposals favoring some form of federal assistance for large-scale public and/or private acquisition of land ranged from creation of a federal revolving fund to aid lesser governments in acquiring land before the development of public facilities, to an assortment of grants and loans to public and private groups interested in the development of new communities. Specific pleas were made in a number of reports for a coherent disposition policy for federal surplus lands.

CHAPTER TWO

A REALISTIC SET
OF ASSUMPTIONS

Our summary of recent efforts to define a national urban growth and land development policy clearly indicates that, apart from developing a consensus that something needs to be done, the nation has not gotten very far. Most of the recommendations of each task force or working group have yet to be converted to legislation, public policy, and/or strategies. Still, every year brings new task forces and new evidence of increased public concern. Perhaps one of the key reasons why a national urban growth and land development policy has remained a somewhat ephemeral subject is the noticeable lack of "toughness" concerning the various assumptions relative to population growth, population distribution, and land consumption accepted by policy-makers and urban analysts. Our own analyses suggest the following:

1. *Considerations related to a national urban growth and/or land development policy should anticipate a population far smaller than that projected in the mid-1960's.*[3]

Certainly, the nation will not approach doubling its 1960 population by the year 2000, as was projected in Census estimates based on high fertility rates. Initial Subcommittee analyses of still incomplete returns from the 1970 Census suggest that less than 80 million new residents will be added to the 1960 population base by the turn of the century.[4]

It is clear, given the above considerations concerning overall population growth, that the nation's land problem should not be in terms of the environmental, social, and economic impact of the land-conversion process. Even if the nation is as productive as demographers projected in the early 1960's, less than 20 million acres will be required, at existing suburban densities, to meet the needs of the new population. While certainly significant in absolute numbers and probable impact, the additional acreage would account for only 1 or 2 percent of the country's land mass. Moreover, an increase would less than double the land now considered in urban use.

2. *Considerations related to a national urban and/or land development policy should be primarily concerned with population growth and distribution internal to metropolitan areas.*

Nearly 85 percent of the net population increase in the United States since 1960 has occurred in metropolitan areas. Urban areas whose size ranged from 200,000 to 2,000,000 proved to be the strongest magnets. Conversely, most areas whose residents numbered less than 50,000 reflected a small net out-migration, while those over 2,000,000 grew only slightly in terms of percentage.[5]

More than six out of every ten Americans now live in metropolitan areas; the dominance of these areas as the favored habitat of most Americans should continue in the foreseeable future. Indeed, close to 80 percent of all new population growth between now and the year 2000 will probably occur within their borders. Even if some of the more optimistic projections of New Town advocates come true, they will only house approximately one out of five new inhabitants estimated to arrive between now and the year 2000.[6]

Migration apparently contributed relatively few people to the number of new people living in metropolitan areas during the 1960's. Most domestic migrants come from small towns and cities rather than rural areas.

3. *Considerations related to a national urban and/or land development policy should focus primarily on the differential growth patterns (and their implications) now occurring between central city and suburban areas.*

Most Americans apparently favor living in suburbia. Indeed, practically all the increase in metropolitan population over the past decade has occurred in the suburbs. More than one half of all metropolitan households now live there. Close to nine out of every ten inhabitants of metropolitan areas will reside there in the foreseeable future either by choice or circumstance.

Most black Americans (almost three fourths) now live in metropolitan areas. Although the suburban black population rose by nearly 800,000 during the past decade, blacks comprised only 5 percent of the total suburban population in 1970.[7] Close to four out of every five blacks still live in the central cities of their respective metropolitan areas. If the present trend continues, nearly two fifths of the total number of people living in central cities will be black and the population of an increasing number of older cities will be over 50 percent black by 1985. Unfortunately, a positive correlation exists between racial concentration, concentration of low-income households, and substandard housing.

Clearly, present political, institutional, and economic constraints make it difficult to conceive of strategies that will significantly affect current migration patterns, the dominance of metropolitan areas, the attraction of suburbs to the most affluent or near-affluent households, and the concentration of blacks in older central cities.

CHAPTER THREE

THE CONVERSION PROCESS

Many significant knowledge gaps remain concerning key aspects of the urbanization process. For example, we do not yet know the optimum size of regions, metropolitan areas, and/or local communities, particularly if optimum is defined in human as well as in economic terms. Neither do we have a firm handle on such often discussed subjects as the proper form and size of metropolitan areas or the most efficient relation among the various users of land. Further, life styles and behavior patterns of most American households are not subject to easy prediction and often overwhelm public and private planning efforts aimed at influencing them.

This Subcommittee, partly because of the backgrounds of its members and partly because of its general mandate from ACHUD, specifically limited its attention to the processes associated with the conversion of vacant land to developed status, and the implications thereof for the cost and rationing of land among competitive uses.

FROM RURAL TO URBAN USE

Nearly 2 million acres of land were converted from rural to non-agricultural special uses between 1950 and 1960.[8] Of this total, over one half million acres were direct additions to urban places and reflected the increasing geographic spread or fringe extension of most metropolitan areas. Although this Subcommittee's review of still in-

12

complete data for the 1960–1970 period suggests a slightly lower net addition of acreage in more recent years to urban place categories, gross figures still testify to the continued vitality of the conversion and expansion process.

Surprisingly, we know little about how the conversion process functions or its impact on the rationing of land among competitive urban land use needs or demands. Data concerning the amount of land transferred by the bulldozer from farm to urban use, for example, remains imprecise and only valuable as indications of gross national or metropolitan trends. Similarly, we do not yet understand the complex interrelationship between land uses and changing land prices. Consequently, our knowledge of the possible impact of land costs on selected land uses (e.g., housing for low-income families) remains at an embryonic stage.

EFFECT ON LAND PRICES

Much of the attention of those who have studied the conversion process has been focused on the rapid rise in raw land prices in and on the fringe of metropolitan areas.[9] The President's Committee on Urban Housing, for example, reported that "while the price of raw land has roughly doubled in major metropolitan areas . . . between 1950 and 1965, in areas of particularly rapid growth . . . prices have gone up five fold. . . ."[10]

After comparing the prices of land ripe for development, Schmidt[11] estimated that the conversion of rural land to urban use resulted in an 1,800 percent appreciation (Table 1)—certainly, more than necessary to bring land into urban circulation.

Recent studies offer evidence that, over the past two decades, undeveloped land in areas ripe for development has increased about 10 to 15 percent a year in value (in deflated dollars). This rate of increase is more than five times that recorded annually in the consumer price index (1 or 2 percent per year). Perhaps as relevant, at least for those interested in basing policy on exceptions, anecdotal evidence is available illustrating price increases far above the average in most rapidly growing sectors of most metropolitan areas.[12]

Generally, prices of land in the metropolitan ring have grown at

TABLE 1   Suburban Raw Land Price Appreciation above Farm Land Prices in Selected U.S. Cities, 1964[13]

City	(1) Suburban Price/Acre	(2) Farm Price/Acre	(3) Appreciation (1) − (2)	Percent Appreciation over Farm Value (3) − (2) × 100
Atlanta, Ga.	$ 1,791	$127	$ 1,664	1,310
Berkeley, Cal.	10,614	460	10,154	3,307
Cincinnati, Ohio	3,696	282	3,412	1,212
Dallas, Texas	7,277	108	7,169	6,638
Harrisburg, Pa.	2,255	222	2,033	916
Minneapolis, Minn.	2,160	168	1,992	1,186
Orlando, Fla.	3,089	307	2,782	906
Portland, Ore.	4,078	99	3,979	4,019
Syracuse, N.Y.	2,600	165	2,435	1,476
Washington, D.C.	5,785	365	5,420	1,485

a more rapid pace than land in central cities or land outside the sphere of urban growth pressures (Table 2). As Table 2 suggests, prices in the metropolitan ring grew in the aggregate at a rate almost one third faster than those of land in central cities and close to two thirds faster than those of land in nonmetropolitan areas.

It is clear that land prices have risen significantly. Yet the phenomenon of excessively rising prices seems, as implied above, limited to

TABLE 2   Land Price Indexes for Nonmetropolitan, Metropolitan Ring, and Central City Areas, United States, 1952–1966 (1952=100)[14]

Year	Nonmetropolitan	Metropolitan Ring of SMSA	Central City
1952	100	100	100
1953	99	135	117
1954	104	143	123
1955	111	180	145
1956	121	200	160
1957	129	230	180
1958	141	250	195
1959	149	270	209
1960	153	290	220
1961	162	310	236
1962	170	325	250
1963	182	345	265
1964	195	360	280
1965	211	370	290
1966	225	390	309

select growth areas and acreage within growth areas. For example, national trend data suggest that, while total land value in this country increased considerably in absolute dollars between 1956 and 1966, the annual rates of change ranged from only 5.5 percent[15,16] to 7.8 percent. Similarly, and perhaps more relevant to this Subcommittee's work, vacant urban lots underwent an annual average price increase of 7.6 percent and farm property only 5.5 percent. In effect, it appears that,

> . . . variation in tax rates and possible returns from alternative investments . . . cannot fall much short of the approximately six percent annual increment in per property land values. . . . When the burden of illiquidity is added, *it is clear that holders of vacant land as a group are not making excessive capital gains.* To whatever extent excessive speculative gains create a problem, it is restricted to particular localities or categories of land. These *indeed* are the most critical. . . .[17] [emphasis added by Subcommittee]

UNDERSTANDING THE LAND MARKET

Unfortunately, we still must rely on sketchy empirical evidence to understand the functioning of the land market, particularly the intensity of the various factors that determine the demand for and supply of land in specific locales and the relation between these factors and the price of land. We do know that, while the supply of metropolitan land—like demand—is elastic to some extent, the price of individual sites is fixed by a relatively small portion of the total supply of land in the metropolitan area. Even for these sites, however, pressures relative to supply and demand do not play themselves out in a perfect market.

No longer can we assume, as once was the case, that the price of raw land is primarily a reflection of the price of agricultural land plus readily defined development costs and one or possibly two profit centers.[18] Surveys undertaken by this Subcommittee, combined with the more intensive studies of others, lend support to the view that a number of intermediary owners may stand between the farmer and the final user of land. It is getting more difficult, in many instances, to separate dealers from developers or speculators from farmers.

By and large, sellers and buyers of land appear to be neither organized nor well informed concerning relevant demand and supply factors in their respective market areas. Yet, it is their individual judgments concerning the present value of future income from specific land holdings that primarily define the boundaries of the land market and make the market an exceedingly risky endeavor for many participants. Survival for both buyers and sellers depends, obviously, on their respective abilities to identify the "right" discount rate–that is, the rate at which to capitalize the projected annual net income from a piece of property. This discount rate must reflect personal decisions concerning the potential return on alternate investments and the impact of alternative decisions on tax positions. As important, it must also reflect observations relative to differential and shifting population pressures and the anticipated level and timing of public investment for infrastructure. In effect, to be successful, a dealer must become a good, if intuitive, economist, planner, and sociologist. Clearly, as shown by the data presented earlier, not too many make it.

VARIATIONS IN PRICE

In retrospect, we seem to have accepted all too easily the view that land values are primarily a function of accessibility to and from the central city (theoretically, the "highest and best use") of a metropolitan area and declined in a somewhat uniform manner as one proceeded from the center of that city to the fringe. Certainly, the desire to minimize transportation costs stimulates a demand for the limited number of close-in sites and, thus, stimulates land prices. Yet several recent observers correctly suggest that other factors unrelated to the trade-off between distance and land costs may also affect the pattern of land prices observed in metropolitan areas.[19]

No simple hierarchical model of land values leading from the central business district (CBD) to fringe areas now suffices to explain the differentials in land prices found in most areas. While the CBD retains a strong hold, accumulated evidence indicates that, as incomes rise, many households prefer a longer and more expensive journey to work if they can secure more amenities and larger sites. In the same context, accessibility to the CBD is not an important factor for those families who want a home near a job, shopping, or services located in suburbia. Clearly, such families do not compete for sites near the CBD.

PUBLIC POLICY AND LAND PRICES

Many often disconnected actions taken by public bodies help either
to provide or to set the context within which buyers and sellers make
decisions concerning the acquisition, rentention, or disposition of
land. Like so many other seemingly significant factors affecting the
land market, our knowledge of the impact of public actions rests
primarily on anecdotes and narrowly focused noncomparable analyses. Some of these public actions are reviewed below.

Capital Gains Tax

Although many have speculated about the impact of the capital gains
tax, we know little about its actual effect on the motivations of land
owners and buyers. For example, while we can readily surmise that
individuals in high-income brackets or corporations find land an
attractive investment (given their ability to shelter from taxes about
one half the gain secured from the sale of land), we cannot say with
certainty how much land is actually purchased for this reason. Shifts
from private to corporate ownership, while noticeable in some
sectors of some metropolitan areas, do not yet appear to be a common
phenomenon. Similarly, data about the income of individuals owning
land in metropolitan areas are fragmentary. Finally, the extent to
which the capital gains tax is acknowledged in the complex and personal opportunity cost equations of land-holders is not clear. As a
result, we cannot define the impact of the capital gains tax either on
the choice of discount rates or on decisions concerning land disposition. Analysis is made more complex because of the possible trade-
offs between the capital gains tax and the deduction provisions of the
federal income tax.

Differential Tax and Assessments

For many years in many locations, land has been assessed at a lower
percentage of value than have structures. Some have attributed this
to the difficulty—political as well as economic—of establishing the
market value of land about to be converted to urban use; others, to
the various depreciation provisions in the federal tax laws that have
made it advantageous to shift value from land to buildings. Recently,

partly in response to urgings of those concerned with preservation of open space and agricultural land, a number of states have legalized differential patterns of assessments both for particular types of land (e.g., agricultural and residential) and for land and buildings. The amount of land that is underassessed in any given sector for any particular metropolitan area is difficult to estimate; similarly, implications of this underassessment remain more the subject of fantasy than reasoned discussion. It should be recognized, however, that despite the relatively low mileage rates for the tax on land, the actual tax may run anywhere from 20 to 35 percent of the annual income from the property.[20]

Development of Infrastructure

Public investments for highways and water and sewer lines affect the value of immediately proximate land, as well as the timing of the development of such land.

Freeways Conversations with developers and state officials suggest that the value of land abutting new freeways may increase anywhere from two to fifty times its value just prior to and during the development period and that land near interchanges may escalate in value at an even faster rate.[21] Other more extensive studies suggest a range of similar increases in value.[22] What we do not accurately know is the effect of freeway development on land values and/or development some distance from the freeway, particularly if the freeway serves to open up a sizable supply of land for new development. Similarly, we cannot yet gage with accuracy the ability of a freeway to create a land market where sizable market restraints existed prior to freeway development. Finally, hard and comparable data concerning the variations in land values between freeway interchanges are limited.

Water and Sewer Development of major water and sewer lines capable of serving suburban or fringe areas also had led to higher land values in some areas and to a more rapid rate of conversion. The experiences of members of this Subcommittee and interviews with a cross section of developers indicate that access to water and sewer lines increases fringe or suburban vacant land values anywhere from two to seven times the value prior to such access. More formal studies prepared by others provide similar data concerning the impact of water and sewer lines.

As with highways, we need more policy-relevant information about the impact of water and sewer lines on land values and land conversion. While several studies point to an increase in market activity after the development of such lines, few studies suggest the impact of such lines in areas in which demand was low or absent prior to development. Similarly, no studies provide comparable information about the effect of water and sewer facilities on land values some distance from such facilities.

Zoning

Short-term benefits or possible costs are conferred on some land owners when local governments designate the uses of land. Discussions of these costs and benefits are generally based on loose generalizations rather than careful analyses.

We know, for example, that, in one rapidly growing area of the country, the price of land zoned for "twin housing" was almost twice that of land zoned for single-family uses. Similarly, the price of land zoned for row housing was more than double the price of land zoned for single-family uses.[23] A survey undertaken by this Subcommittee gave evidence that land rezoned or upgraded from single-family to multiple-family use, or from agricultural to a "higher use," generally showed a significant increase in value. Estimates ranged from about twice to many times the base value or the value just prior to the change in zoning. It seemed clear, however, that land values would not have increased substantially if a demand had not existed prior to the change in zoning for the new use.

A reasonably stable zoning ordinance permits projection of the future use of land and thus is one of the key factors in calculating prospective buyers and sellers of land. No doubt, in areas of reasonably rapid growth, a tough ordinance limiting development would tend to lower the short-term value of land; similarly, a more flexible or easily amended ordinance would increase expectations for future income from land and thus its asking price.

Assuredly, zoning of one type or another influences one's perceptions of land values. Experts are made when their guesstimates luckily conform to reality. We, unfortunately, do not have good national data on the impact of zoning or zoning changes on the elasticity of land consumption and associated land prices. Except in a general sense, we have only sketchy information on the many factors leading to the establishment of or change in alternate types of zoning ordinances. Analyses in the popular press have been confined primarily to supposedly "exclusionary" local land use policies—that is, practices such as excluding multi-family uses or maintaining requirements for large lots per single-family unit. Even here our knowledge is marginal. For example, we do not know the extent to which exclusionary practices are based on legitimate fiscal opportunity costing by local governments, or on local discriminatory practices.

INTENSITY OF LAND USE AND COST OF SERVICES

Although the supposed excessive development costs associated with the present conversion process have been described by many, hard and comparable data to support such a conclusion are scarce. Beyond the truism that high-density residential areas consume less land than do low-density areas, certainty vanishes (Table 3). Those who criticize "sprawl" have not effectively responded to those who argue that: (a) the present pattern of development not only conforms to consumer desires but *may* be an effective way of holding land from premature development; (b) while initial development costs may be higher, subsequent strategic "in fill" may in the end actually result

TABLE 3   Land Required To House One Million People for Various Residential Types[a]

Type of Units	No. of Acres
High-rise	4,474
Medium-rise	6,734
Garden	15,037
Townhouse	20,964
Single-family	111,111

[a]Source: Kamm.[24]

in lower total costs than would have been possible with more planned or ordered development; (c) the present pattern of development provides more options with respect to the acquisition of cheaper land than would a more regulated and orderly one; and (d) most development costs are "insensitive" to the form of development.

Data presented to support cluster development generally fail to portray the implications of such development on other than direct infrastructure costs. For example, most studies do not go beyond estimating cost "savings" for specific projects in specific areas developed during specific time periods. Very few consider the impact of cluster development on community or areawide development costs or operating costs related to alternative development patterns (Tables 4 and 5).

DEFINING THE IMPACT

The Subcommittee sought definitive answers to questions about the impact of the conversion process and rising land prices. Although a necessary prerequisite to development of urban growth strategies, these answers were not easy to secure from existing studies or government officials. Popular use of descriptive but value-laden terms, such as "sprawl," "slurb," and "scatteration," does little for understanding. Similarly, to attribute to the land conversion process much of

TABLE 4   Cost Estimates for a 300-Acre Subdivision Development, Ville Du Parc, Wisconsin, under Conventional and Clustered Development Plans, 1962[a]

Items	Conventional	Clustered
Sewer and water	$ 439,770	$258,490
Streets	104,000	68,120
Storm drains	220,140	56,600
Engineering, etc.	41,178	26,725
Sidewalks, hydrants	51,160	10,672
Land	360,000	360,000
Total development cost	1,216,248	780,607
Cost per lot	4,807	2,891

[a]Source: *Journal of Homebuilding.*[25]

TABLE 5   Land and Public Service Costs, per Thousand, for Estimated
Development by 1985, Howard County, Maryland[a]

Cost Item	Model I: Sprawl	Model II: Partly Sprawl, Partly Clustered	Model III: Closely Clustered
Area of land (acres)			
Residential	49,000	33,900	22,400
Commercial	3,150	2,750	2,450
Industrial	9,000	6,575	4,750
Water utilities installations	$65,011	$47,110	$32,068
Sewer utilities installations	83,941	62,777	38,693
Road installations	54,745	38,072	25,746
Road maintenance, 1965–1985	20,548	14,773	10,509
County acquisition of parks and open space	534	1,689	2,384
County acquisition of school sites	3,412	2,250	800
School bus operation, 1965–1985	23,965	15,254	9,031

[a]Source: *Howard County, 1985.*[26]

the blame for the fact that our suburbs are, by and large, colored
white and our cities black, belies very real class and caste divisions
apparently endemic to the national character.

HOUSING

Lurking behind most discussions on the need for a national growth
or land development policy is one's perception of "the housing
problem." Those concerned with "sprawl" and "slurb" view "un-
controlled, haphazard" development of housing units as the central
development problem; those concerned with the increasing trend
toward black cities and white suburbs view housing discrimination
as the problem; to others, the disparity between housing revenue
and services is the core development problem; and those concerned
with improving the "quality" of urban life generally stress the existence and clustering of substandard housing conditions as the central development problem.

Certainly, the general rise in land values described on page 14 has
affected the ability of many families to secure adequate shelter. The
fact that the median price of new conventionally built housing approaches $30,000, and the minimal rental for new apartments is

rarely below $175 per month, suggests that one need not be a trained housing economist to know that new housing is "off limits" to the majority of American households. Even modest increases in real housing costs exacerbate the situation, whether they are from increases in the cost of land or other cost components.

Until recently, the cost of raw land has increased in percentage more rapidly than any other housing cost component (Figure 1). Yet, despite this fact, raw land rarely exceeds 15 percent of total housing costs and, in most instances, ranges from only 2 to 10 percent of the total cost of a unit. Further, while often-quoted FHA data illustrate ever increasing site–value cost relations (Table 6), such data do not explain the relationship between raw land and development costs or the impact of changes in lot size or the level and quality of land improvements on land prices.

To date, little research has been undertaken relating shifts in income to changes in demand for lot sizes. Most studies do not separate the demand for different lot sizes from the demand for suburban housed of different sizes and costs. One 1963 analysis of land prices in the San Francisco Bay area estimates that close to half of the site-cost increase was due to the increased quality of site improvements and the increased size of lots.[29] Other studies in other areas corroborate the significant influence of these two factors on overall site costs.

Several developers interviewed during the course of this study suggested that development costs have kept pace or had exceeded the rate of increase for raw land. Presently, development costs in typical low-density developments seem to range from two to four times raw land costs. Many of those interviewed called attention to the fact that, in absolute dollars, costs related to site development are often far more important to the total cost of housing than the cost of raw land. Elimination of land costs from the average FHA-insured unit would provide less impact on total housing costs than a 1 percent reduction in present financing costs.

ALLOCATION OF LAND FOR DIFFERENT USES

As the previous section indicates, land costs are not the key problem associated with efforts to reduce housing costs. But such costs and the conversion process that led to them have served to allocate land

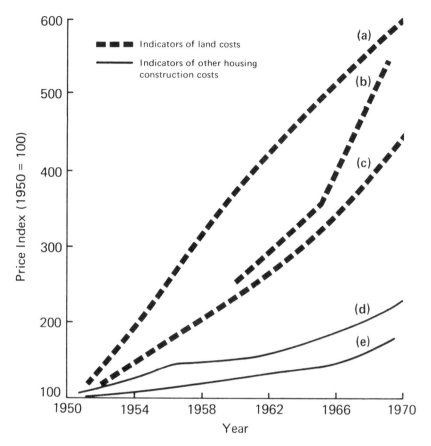

FIGURE 1   Comparative trends in land costs and other housing construction costs (1950-1970). (a) Land price index for metropolitan ring of SMSA (Table 6, column 2). Adjusted to 1950 = 100, 1966-1970 extrapolated. (b) NAHB membership survey report on cost of "typical finished lot" (Table 3). Position on scale estimated. (c) Market price of sites for FHA Sec. 203(b) mortgages (Table 2). Adjusted to 1950 = 100. (d) Estimated property value for FHA Sec. 203(b) mortgages, less market price of site (Table 2). Adjusted to 1950 = 100. (e) Boech residential construction cost index from HUD *1969 Statistical Yearbook*. Adjusted to 1950 = 100.

Source: Kamm.[28]

among different uses in a manner seemingly inconsistent with stated national objectives. To illustrate:

1. The absence of clear-cut state or metropolitan guidelines for the use of land and the lack of a coordinated strategy for the devel-

TABLE 6   FHA One-Family New Home Transactions [Sec. 203(b)] [a]

Year	Site–Value Percentage	Price of Site (per ft^2)
1950	12.0	–
1960	16.7	–
1965	20.0	–
1966	20.2	.54
1967	19.9	.59
1968	20.8	.65
1969	20.4	.68
1970	20–21	77–90

[a]Source: U.S. Department of Housing and Urban Development.[27]

opment of highways and water and sewer lines leave often competing local governments in the primary public role of influencing private market decisions concerning the acquisition or disposition of land. For example, land use regulations that aim, as indicated earlier, at either eliminating certain types of housing completely or increasing the costs of all types of housing are but one way in which local governments modify and direct allocations of land among different users. Certainly, the quest for industry by local jurisdictions (related, in part, to local reliance on the property tax) has affected the use of land, often resulting in either freezing land in unused open space because of the lack of demand, or the location of an industry in areas where there is no employee housing. Differential patterns of assessment and/or taxation are another way in which jurisdictions have altered the allocation and distribution of land among competing users, even though they are not always aware of the impact of their actions.

2. The quick opening of relatively less expensive land in suburban and fringe areas has sometimes negatively affected the value of land and buildings nearer to some of the older cities and suburban areas. Existence of dead areas in most larger Eastern cities—areas not always the "worst" sections of town—and the presence of unused suburban land in some Western and Midwestern cities testify to this phenomenon.

3. When builders cannot increase density, they intuitively multiply the land price by a factor of four or five to set the cost of a housing unit. Thus, a nominal increase in the land cost can cause a major increase in the ultimate cost of housing to the consumer. Families

whose incomes fail to keep pace with increased costs are frozen out of certain locales in suburban and fringe areas.

4. Misinformation often enters the calculations of the numerous unorganized buyers and sellers who collectively constitute the "local market." Decisions to hold land ripe for development for a better deal, while maintaining open space, may increase immediate price pressures on nearby land and skew land development patterns.

CHAPTER FOUR

ALLOCATION CRITERIA, SELECTED CRITERIA, SELECTED DEMONSTRATIONS, AND NEEDED RESEARCH

This Subcommittee has consciously tried to avoid easy acceptance of conventional wisdoms concerning the land conversion process. For example, we have seriously questioned general beliefs about both the impact of and the benefits accruing to the land speculator. Similarly, we have called attention to the limited impact land costs have on overall housing costs, and we briefly alluded to the possible benefits, as well as the costs, of sprawl.

We have also attempted to call attention to the deficiencies in the nation's knowledge of the conversion process and its impact on development. Presently, available analyses have failed to answer significant policy-relevant questions about the key variables affecting the conversion process and their relation to land prices, housing costs, and the distribution of land uses.

Because we clearly do not know enough as a nation and because what we do know suggests that *land development problems—while important—are not yet crucial, this Committee is hesitant, based on its brief reconnaissance, to recommend "national" policy for urban growth or land development.* Indeed, even if more information were available, we doubt, given the pluralism reflected in the nation's goals and varied institutions, that it would be possible to devise a federally prescribed master plan or a federally defined comprehensive and coordinated urban growth policy dealing in more than general terms with population growth and distribution and land use.

Moreover, even if it were possible, we doubt that it would be wise and proper.

The Subcommittee is convinced, however, that firm and consistent criteria can be developed to guide the federal government as it allocates funds to meet urban growth and land development needs. It is also prepared to recommend, apropos of its mandate, immediate development of several "live" demonstrations, to improve the ability of state and metropolitan jurisdictions to successfully influence the land conversion process, and initiation of a policy and program relevant research program directed at providing, for the first time, a clear understanding of the land conversion process.

CRITERIA FOR ALLOCATION OF FUNDS

Earlier, we commented on the marginal role most state and metropolitan groups played in the land conversion process. Certainly . . . "the absence of clear-cut state or metropolitan guidelines for the use of land . . . grant often competing local governments the primary public role in influencing private market decisions concerning the acquisition or disposition of land." Most local plans and capital-improvement programs do not reflect areawide objectives and strategies concerning the relationship between city and suburb and among various land uses or the development of housing and appropriate community services for low-income households in suburban and fringe areas.

HUD deserves credit for its current efforts to strengthen the capacity of state, metropolitan, and local governments to resolve planning and community development problems. These efforts would be reinforced considerably if the federal government granted priority in the allocation of funds, including funds for housing and community development to:

1. those states and metropolitan areas that have prepared or are in the process of preparing appropriate areawide development plans and coordinated development strategies;

2. local projects consistent with areawide plans and approved by appropriate metropolitan planning groups;

3. large-scale projects that exceed state- or metropolitan-defined minimum requirements;

4. those state and metropolitan areas that have, in their areawide plans, responded to the needs of low- and moderate-income families; and

5. projects that respond to the needs of low- and moderate-income households.

DEMONSTRATIONS

Most state, metropolitan, and local governments have not been able to define or carry out consistent objectives concerning land development through the coordinated use of their powers.

Indeed, few state, metropolitan, or local governments have the capacity to influence the land conversion process in other than an *ad hoc*, limited, and often disruptive way. Further, no single federal strategy is available to help build the management and planning capacity of lesser governments. Certainly, increased suburban dominance of state legislatures and black dominance of central cities do not suggest an easy political path toward developing the institutional capacity of state, metropolitan, and local governments.

The Subcommittee proposes that the federal government initiate a number of carefully designed demonstration programs in a selected group of states and metropolitan areas.[30] Each program would be directed at defining appropriate strategies to increase the capacity of state, metropolitan, and local governments either to influence or to participate in the land conversion process.

A SINGLE MANAGEMENT AND PLANNING GRANT DEMONSTRATION

We propose experimentation with a single management and planning grant and possibly a single point of entry for all federal funds concerned with land and community development in carefully selected states and metropolitan areas. While HUD's 701 planning assistance program is perhaps the most visible, there are presently 10 to 20 separate federal planning grants aimed at "building local capacity" to guide land development or community building processes more effectively. Each contains different funding formulas, administrative guidelines, recipients, and beneficiaries. In effect, because of uncoordinated and often inconsistent guidelines governing their use, federal planning aids have not appeared to improve the ability of most local governments to affect the land conversion process.

Various proposals, some of them Administration generated, are now before Congress for statutory consolidation. It is probable that these proposals will require much debate and time before approval. Our examination of the statutory and administrative criteria associated with present programs suggests that it is possible to begin now to move toward the packaging of one basic management and planning grant at the federal level.

We propose that this be done. To the extent that statutes permit, a consolidated grant should be immediately offered to state and metropolitan groups willing to use it to develop appropriate 5- and 1-year land development programs linked to complementing capital improvement and capital budget programs. Such funds should be provided only to responsible chief executives and not, as is commonly done, allocated to separate agencies and departments. Initiation of areawide land planning should be followed by a federal commitment of appropriate aid.

Unlike most present federal aid, assistance should be assured for at least a 5-year period and be free of most federal criteria. Continuous evaluation should be made of the effect of this type of planning assistance on the ability of state and metropolitan governments to secure adequate staff, to produce suitable local land development plans, to more effectively achieve locally defined development objectives, and to maximize state and local expenditures for infrastructure.

ALTERNATE INCENTIVES TO INCREASE SUBURBAN WILLINGNESS TO ACCEPT LOW-INCOME HOUSEHOLDS

We have noted the difficult fiscal decisions many suburban areas must make because of the present reliance on the property tax and the haphazard, unclear distribution of responsibilities between federal, state, and local governments for basic education, welfare, and health services. More than one local government official told us that "the cost of services for the average family is three to four times what they pay in taxes." Data reviewed by this Committee seem to bear this out. While average annual service costs run from $300 to $500 per person, yield from the property tax does not exceed $300–$500 per family.

The potential impact of the addition of a significant number of large or poor families causes many mayors and managers to anticipate serious cash flow problems and to resist throwing out the welcome mat. When discriminatory antiblack or antipoor feelings are also present, they add to the pressures for large lot zoning and restrictions on multiple-family units.

Because adequate analyses have not been made concerning the distribution of service costs between and among levels of government and the relationship of such costs to local taxes and transfer payments, it is difficult to separate legitimate fiscal actions from discrimination. Many propose denying federal funds to communities clearly practicing discrimination; while laudable in principle, we doubt that this will have much real impact. Statutory problems aside, federal programs generally amount to less than 5 percent of most suburban communities' operating budgets.[31]

We propose early implementation of a limited demonstration program. This program should offer to selected counties and municipalities, willing to revise present restrictive land use regulations, a planning grant covering costs associated with amending land controls; preference among existing housing assistance programs; and, presuming congressional approval, a development grant equal to the estimated differences between local tax yields and additional service costs that result from new lower-income population.

The demonstration effort should be structured to test the impact of such incentives on community willingness to absorb varying numbers of lower-income families. It should also be structured to provide empirical evidence concerning alternatives to traditional restrictive zoning and subdivision regulations; the impact of a planned influx of lower-income families on a range of community services; and the effectiveness of alternate types of federal assistance in absorbing higher community service costs that, ostensibly, result from in-migration of lower-income families.

DEVELOPMENT OF LAND BANKS

Public control of land has in recent times been favored by many as the most direct and effective way of achieving several ostensibly key public objectives relative to the use of land. Therefore, creation of land banks to achieve public ownership of land has recently attracted the favor of some. Such banks usually would assume the posture of a state, metropolitan, or municipal corporation. They would be granted powers of eminent domain, land development (particularly related to site preparation), and land disposal. In general, their functions encompass the following:

1. Advance acquisition of land for public purposes, including development of housing for low- and moderate-income households, open space, new communities, etc.

2. Acquisition and disposal of land to influence its price in metropolitan markets or submarkets

3. Acquisition and disposal of land to permit the public sector to *recapture* values created primarily by the public

Unfortunately, most land bank models have been borrowed from an irrelevant European experience. We have little evidence about how land banks would work in our metropolitan areas. Instead of recommending national policy at this time, we prefer to urge the initiation of specific demonstrations in select metropolitan areas. Such demonstrations would be structured to test: (a) the consistency of land bank objectives. We should examine whether the public "rationing of land" inherent in the land bank concept is compatible with provision of land at reasonable costs for low- and moderate-income households; (b) the needed scale and timing of land acquisition to provide leverage on market prices; (c) the ability of land banks to recapture publicly created values. We should use the demonstration to develop an equitable accounting system able to define publicly created values resulting from public action; (d) the differential between public and private holding costs and the impact of such differentials on initial land bank objectives. We feel that only a marginal difference may exist between public and private holding costs. Proposed land banks should test whether aggregate debt service costs would deny most land banks freedom to price land consistently with legitimate locally defined social objectives; (e) the political viability of land banks. It is assumed that proposed land banks, particularly those with extraterritorial jurisdictions, will run into political difficulties with existing public jurisdictions. We should use the demonstration to test the intensity and impact of these assumed political problems.

The federal government should examine the possibility of providing the following types of assistance to facilitate such demonstrations:

1. Grants for general land bank planning and feasibility analysis
2. Grants for general land bank staffing assistance
3. Guarantees for debt financing or direct loans for land acquisition
4. Direct subsidies to cover holding costs
5. Coordinated use of existing federal aid to develop infrastructure

EXTRATERRITORIAL[32] LAND ACQUISITION

Results of land bank demonstrations suggested above, in addition to responding to unanswered questions relating to land banks, will help to define the appropriateness of extraterritorial acquisition of land by government entities. Many of the questions raised in the discussion of land banks are also relevant to proposals to provide extraterritorial acquisition of land to states, metropolitan areas, and cities. For example, if the scale of contemplated land acquisition is large, problems related to the impact on land prices might occur and must be resolved. Similarly, problems related to initial and long-term holding costs must be anticipated and attended to. Finally, and perhaps most crucial, if extraterritorial land acquisition is encouraged for the purposes of developing low- and moderate-income housing alternatives, we should acknowledge the fact that infrastructure and preservicing costs may be more expensive than similar efforts in already developed areas; that transportation costs may force a burden on most occupants; that we may be reinventing the ghetto in a less attractive environment; that we may be further exacerbating jurisdictional problems without significant pay-offs among municipalities; and that cities, in concentrating on new housing, may be restricting unnecessarily their ability to provide more standard housing options within the existing housing stock.

We believe, as with land banks, that the nation is not yet ready to create national policy. Because there are no apparent legal impediments to extending extraterritorial land acquisition and development and disposal powers to lesser governments, we propose the encouragement of a limited number of demonstrations involving states, metropolitan area groups, and cities. These demonstrations should be limited initially to preparing sites for new housing developments near job generators. The range of assistance required would be similar in nature to that proposed for the land bank.

DISPOSITION OF FEDERAL LAND

Close to 6 million acres of federally owned vacant land exist in the nation's metropolitan areas. Despite rhetoric favoring the disposition of federal land for urban use, no complete inventory exists to define both the location of federal land and its anticipated use.

Initial Subcommittee surveys suggest that, in many communities, federal holdings command strategic locations with respect to local development needs. Their conversion to local ownership—consistent with legitimate federal interests—would, in many instances, facilitate demonstration programs relative to local government land banks and extraterritorial land acquisition programs; strategies concerning recoupment of publicly created values; alternatives pertaining to the leasing, rather than the disposition, of publicly owned land; and alternatives concerning new town-in-towns and open space—recreation strategies.

As a prelude to a possible new high priority demonstration federal surplus land release program, the Subcommittee recommends the initiation of a complete survey of federally owned vacant lands in and around major metropolitan areas. This survey should describe the extent and location of federal lands. It also should describe present and contemplated use and federal agency interests. The burden should be placed on respective agencies to prove why their holdings should not be considered for possible conversion to state, metropolitan, or local government ownership, particularly if such conversion meets locally defined and federally approved objectives for land development.

In addition to quick development of the above survey, the Subcommittee recommends that the federal government re-evaluate experiences with the 5-year-old "new town-in-town" or surplus land disposition program. Clearly, early expectations associated with this program have not been met. Cities have not been able either to develop on "surplus federal land . . . new communities," or to use federally disposed land to test innovative planning, development, or land use controls.

Discussions with federal and local officials and perusal of the literature suggest severe problems with the surplus land program. These include:

1. The lack of a consistent pricing policy reflecting overall development needs and community resources

2. Failure to achieve a coordinated and consistent policy to guide federal reviews of locally conceived planning and development programs

3. The lack of a coordinated policy for the use of appropriate federal funds for planning and community development purposes

4. Failure to define a consistent disposition policy concerning ownership, leasing, and reversion rights

RECOUPMENT OF PUBLICLY CREATED LAND VALUES

Earlier we commented on the fact that public action related to highway development, water and sewer construction, zoning, etc., results in large increases in the value of land owned by some and possible decreases in the value of land owned by others. In the economist's terms, an "externality in economic values" has been created. As with most externalities, land values have not been affected in an equal or proportionate manner throughout most metropolitan areas.

Some have argued, often vociferously, that it is unfair for land owners to reap the benefits of public investment; others, less concerned with equity or justice, have merely called attention to the possibility that it might be bad business and bad politics for public agencies to avoid attempts to recapture the rewards of their own actions.

Despite the *prima facie* merits of arguments favoring public recoupment of publicly created increases in land values, local governments have not been successful in initiating appropriate strategies. In effect, it has proved easier to advocate recoupment than to devise equitable ways to determine the extent of price increases and the responsibility for such increases, to identify owners who will receive "special" treatment, and to assess the benefit (and costs) of public actions on contiguous land.

As important, it has also proved difficult to develop recoupment programs that pass constitutional, political, and financial tests. For example, principles accepted for condemning land for public purposes and use have not been extended to the acquisition of land by eminent domain for primarily revenue-producing purposes. Similarly, while the purchase of development rights has won legal acceptance, such purchase has won only limited public support and understanding. Finally, lack of fiscal resources has limited the advance acquisition of land by local government even though it is probably the most direct technique for recouping increases in land value.

There needs to be more examination of the benefits and costs of alternative recoupment programs. The demonstrations, described earlier, concerning extraterritorial land acquisition, land banks, and federal disposition of land should be viewed as an opportunity to define and possibly carry out recoupment strategies. These strategies should include advance acquisition of land, acquisition of less than fee simple rights in land, experimentation with floating zones for certain uses and the subsequent purchase of zoning; and revision and amendment of local assessment and taxation practices.[33]

INCREASED USE OF LEASE PROVISIONS

Most federal or state programs that assist public jurisdictions in acquiring land favor the ultimate sale of such land. These programs buttress already existing fiscal and management pressures to sell vacant land.

The decision to lease or to sell is a highly complicated one, and public agencies are often unable to easily define the essential variables that must be considered before making such a decision. In many respects, the factors to be considered are similar to those entering the opportunity cost equations of private landowners and developers. Only in this instance, the discount rate must (or should) clearly reflect a community's present and future social needs and priorities, as well as its present and anticipated political climate. It seems clear in this regard that leasing, rather than sale, will increase opportunities to implement public plans and to "recapture" positive and control negative externalities. It also seems clear that leasing will increase the public's leverage as a participant in the conversion process.

The federal government should consider means that permit local governments more opportunities, should they desire to take them, to lease rather than sell publicly owned vacant land, including land acquired through urban renewal or through the various programs proposed earlier. For example, lease rather than sale conditions should be considered as relevant attachments to a portion of the land disposed of by the federal government to lesser governments and, subsequently, reflected in federal disposition and pricing procedures in dealing with local governments. Similarly, the federal government should be asked to consider development of alternatives to supplement any possible differences between ground rents and anticipated property tax receipts.

NEW COMMUNITY DEVELOPMENT

The Subcommittee allocated considerable time to a discussion of the merits of new towns because of their place in current national discussions on land problems. Indeed, publicly assisted new community development has been looked on for some time by many influential groups as an important element in a national urban growth strategy. Certainly, Title VII[34] of the Urban Growth and New Community Acts of 1970 represents more than a modest victory for those who have articulated support for federally supported new communities as an alternative to the present land conversion process. Appropriately, therefore, in enacting the legislation, Congress concluded that:

the national welfare requires the encouragement of well-planned, diversified, and economically sound new communities . . .

Response to Title VII

Despite the relative newness of the program, HUD has received over 100 inquiries from developers regarding Title VII benefits. Six project applications already have received commitments for loan guarantees totaling $124.5 million. Reservations for four supplementary grants have been made for close to $1.6 million, and HUD is nearing a decision on at least five applications for special planning assistance grants.

Most new town projects requesting federal assistance are satellite communities—that is, communities internal to, or on the fringe of, metropolitan areas. Of a total of 58 applications and preapplications (including the six insured), as of July 15, 1971, about two thirds were for satellite developments. Another 20 percent were for new town-in-towns and the rest were split between the "free standing" new towns and "add-ons" to smaller towns and cities (growth centers).

The early response to the Title VII program has been impressive. We hope, however, that neither the Administration nor the Congress will oversell the role new communities can play in meeting the serious social and economic problems that confront American society. Our own skepticism concerning the claims of those who would make new communities a primary focus for federal resources and a primary element of national urban policy, leads us to offer the following observations:

1. It is doubtful, given existing resource commitments, whether this nation will see "the creation of one hundred new communities averaging 100,000 population each and ten new communities of at least one million in population"[35] by the turn of the century. However, even if such new communities are developed, they will house less than 10 percent of the nation's total population and, at best, only about 25 percent of the projected increase in population between 1970 and 2000. Further, at existing suburban densities, such proposed new development will consume under 3 million acres land, or less than one eighth of the total land subject to development between now and the twenty-first century.[36]

2. Given consumer preferences for metropolitan residents and the lack of meaningful programs to change these preferences, it is unlikely that a substantial market exists for "free standing" new towns, or new towns built in small growth centers.

3. We question whether scale of development alone will give the necessary leverage to developers currently assumed by cash flow projections for most Title VII new towns. Market uncertainties complemented by heavy front end costs for land and preservicing present heavy risks to developers and public jurisdictions—risks that are only rarely included in discount calculations.

4. We fear that new communities will not be able to play a major role in providing increased housing opportunities for low-income residents of our older cities. Any meaningful attempt to provide low- and moderate-income housing options in new communities (particularly free standing) must be premised on conscious skewing of industrial location patterns—a skewing that appears neither possible nor wise given political and institutional constraints—and on lack of knowledge about the impact of such a policy on older more developed areas. Second, it must rely on heavy subsidies to meet the need for extra (and different) services and the construction of new housing. It may be that more low-income people could secure standard housing with proper services if funds to be allocated for this purpose to new towns were used in metropolitan areas instead and if the strategy were not limited to providing new housing, as is the case in new towns.[37]

5. It is not yet clear whether new communities will result in significant innovations. Most federal agencies, local jurisdictions, and developers have trouble in operationally defining the term. Pressures will increase to make the projects appear to be beneficial and financially feasible. That which has worked in the past may be preferable to that which appears risky and possibly costly. Conservatism may be supported by our lack of understanding of the relation between varied life styles and the environment, as well as by preference for certainty and equity protection.

6. We question whether the range of proposed and soon-to-be proposed new communities will consume less land and reflect a more efficient development pattern than well-planned suburban areas. Initial analyses suggest that overall densities of most approved communities nearly match existing suburban or fringe densities. Further, it seems reasonable to assume that the replication of existing amenity, infrastructure, and services may result in heavy initial outlays and limit, in certain urbanized areas, the ability of the public sector to optimize expenditures already made for existing facilities and services. Also, from a public policy vantage point, present taxing mechanisms offer little hope that the public can recoup much of the funds spent for the amenities and increased services often associated with new towns.[38]

Our primary purpose in recording the above concerns is to secure a more realistic view of what new communities can and cannot achieve. We would not elevate them at this time to a dominant role in national policy. *We would, however, encourage well-defined demonstration efforts*—efforts supported by Title VII.

Our suspicion is that most community building aided under Title VII, given market factors and congressionally imposed tests of financial feasibility, will not be "free standing" communities but, rather, satellite communities. If we are correct, a well-coordinated Title VII program could permit state and metropolitan entities to test alternative responses to needs created by growth. In this respect, they are consistent with our proposals for testing land banks and extraterritorial land acquisition.

Tests of Alternatives and Relationships

Similarly, assuming a reasonable level of federal assistance, the new community program could test several important items on the national housing and community development agenda. Among them are alternate public and private ways to acquire land in fringe areas; the relationship between income and racial distribution patterns and alternate types of merchandising, land use, and community service strategies; linkages between scale of development, density, and costs; and the implications of using "technological advancements" in developing housing infrastructure, and community services.

Acquisition of Land   New community demonstrations should be designed to test the feasibility of state and metropolitan acquisition of land for community development as well as to test the appropriateness of providing private developers with eminent domain powers. Feasibility and appropriateness would be measured, in part, by evidence concerning land and development costs, alternate scale of necessary acquisitions, and timing of land purchases.

Alternate Income and Racial Patterns   A new community effort should mount several well-defined demonstrations aimed at testing the impact of alternate racial and income mixes on merchandising approaches, land use, and community services strategies. Such demonstrations would increase our understanding of the relations among alternate demographic patterns, marketing programs, uses of space, and types of services.

Scale of Development and Density   A new community effort could be structured to provide much needed data on the relations among scale of development, density, general development, and service costs.

Use of Technology   A new community effort could test the relevance of the "new technology" and of community or social service "innovations." Needed benefit–cost studies could be made concerning use of a range of new materials and approaches in the construction of housing; in the development of water and sewer lines; and in the provision of services.

RESEARCH

Several essential research projects deserve early federal support. Their implementation would help generate the necessary theoretical and empirical base on which to define and build a relevant set of federal objectives and a more effective role in the land conversion process. Among those projects, the Subcommittee recommends for immediate consideration the following:

DEVELOPMENT OF A RAW LAND PRICE INDEX

At present, no index comparable to the consumer price index is prepared either on a city-by-city or on a metropolitan area basis, which describes changes in raw land prices. A raw land price index would be a valuable tool to all levels of government desiring to understand and influence the land conversion process; such an index would also help make private decisions to sell, hold, or acquire land conform to more realistic expectations.

   In recommending federal funding to develop this index, we have not underestimated the methodological problems. Unlike many consumer items, comparable land sales are not easily defined. Further, market prices can be easily obscured by the use of complex debt instruments; also, trend data on particular sites are often of limited use given changing property lines, difficulties in separating land value from building value, and varied local assessment practices. Such problems, however, appear amenable to study and the pay-off seems high.

DEVELOPMENT OF ACCEPTED MEANINGS OF COMMONLY USED TERMS FOR LAND CONVERSION

Irrespective of the claims of different users that they have different needs, we regret that no common definitions of such terms as "urban," "rural land," "vacant land," "developed," and "undeveloped land" exist in the lexicon of professionals. We recommend a federal effort to define these as well as other terms and, subsequently, that these new definitions be used in all federal agencies aggregating data on the use of land. Only then, will we attain comparable and usable data of the urbanization process.

DEVELOPMENT OF A FIRMER UNDERSTANDING OF THE PARTICIPANTS IN THE LAND CONVERSION PROCESS AND THE EFFECT OF THEIR PARTICIPATION

We suggested earlier, based on admittedly sketchy and partial evidence, that, in addition to the farmer and the final user of land, many intermediaries appear to be involved in the land conversion process. Each of these intermediaries may be a profit center; each, through additional acquisitions or investment, may change the nature and value of the acreage; and each may consider a range of different factors when making decisions about their land.

It is essential, if we are to understand the conversion process, for us to understand, first, who participates in the process. The federal government should underwrite a comparable set of analyses in several metropolitan areas to describe both the participants and their role and impact over an extended period of time.

DEVELOPMENT OF A BETTER UNDERSTANDING OF THE FACTORS AFFECTING THE PRICE OF LAND AND THEIR RELATIONS

We briefly reviewed the many variables that apparently affect the price of land in metropolitan areas. We also commented on the fact that the distribution of prices in metropolitan areas no longer appears to be rigidly defined by distance from the central business district or the area of ostensibly "highest and best use." Unfortunately, we must still depend on sketchy data and intuition in trying to understand the range and intensity of the ingredients affecting land prices.

The federal government should immediately fund an analysis of the varied components related to the price of land. Such an analysis, to be useful, would include more than one metropolitan area and would compare the effect of demand and supply factors in varied sectors of selected metropolitan areas. Of priority concern should be the development of an operational model able to relate the impact of various public actions (ranging from zoning to tax increases) on the prices of directly affected contiguous and noncontiguous land.

DEVELOPMENT OF A BETTER UNDERSTANDING OF HOW THE PRESENT ARRAY OF FEDERAL, STATE, AND LOCAL TAXES AFFECT LAND CONVERSION AND LAND PRICES

The Subcommittee earlier called attention to the fact that we do not fully understand the impact of the present tax structure on the land market. Emphasis on the encouragement the capital-gains tax gives to speculators seems based more on intuition than reasoned judgment. Similarly, historical efforts to tax land at differential rates (not legitimized in certain states) seem grounded more in ideology than facts.

Despite the fact that many commissions have called for a complete federally supported study of the impact of the present federal, state, and local tax structure on land development, to the best of this Subcommittee's knowledge, none has been completed. We recommend that the federal government immediately fund such a study. Based on its findings, the federal government would be able to judge the impact on land development of several currently popular proposals, including (a) eliminating or amending the capital-gains tax, (b) revising present building depreciation schedules, (c) reliance on a sales or value-added tax to reduce the burden of property taxes, and (d) allocating federal assistance on the basis of tax yield or tax performance.

DEVELOPMENT OF A BETTER UNDERSTANDING OF ASSESSMENT PRACTICES

Recent court cases concerning inequities in the property tax, particularly reliance on the tax to finance educational programs, should strengthen efforts to determine the impact of widely varying local assessment practices. Even within a single metropolitan area, different jurisdictions often value land and buildings differently and apply different assessment ratios and exemption strategies to similar classes of land use. Varying tax rates further complicate the local tax picture and make it difficult to define or compare effective tax yields on either land or buildings.

We recommend that the federal government immediately support an analysis of the effect local assessment and taxing practices have on land development and the distribution of land uses. This analysis should consider the impact on land conversion of several current proposals now in common currency, including (a) consolidating tax and assessment jurisdictions; (b) shifting present local tax burdens to land; (c) attributing use, rather than capital value, to land for assessment purposes; (d) escalating tax and/or assessment responsibility to state or metropolitan groups; (e) alternatives to the property tax at the state and local level; and (f) shifting some of the burden of the property tax to alternative types of federal assistance.

DEVELOPMENT OF NEW TECHNIQUES FOR THE FINANCING OF LAND

Recently, private profit groups have undertaken to emulate FHA and enter the mortgage insurance business. Although "these firms have only recently appeared on the economic scene . . . their part is not trivial . . . Mortgage Guaranty Insurance Corporation [MGIC], the oldest and largest, holds insurance on two percent of the outstanding home mortgage debt and accounts for about six percent of all mortgage insurance in force."[39]

Because it was not within our specific frame of reference, we did not dwell on current ideas concerning the "phasing down of FHA" and the assumption by the private sector of all but the subsidized or special need housing insurance programs. We did, however, consider the relevance of FHA and private sector experiences to current land financing processes—processes that have failed to benefit appreciably from government insurance of mortgage financing of basic housing costs.

It is clear that apart from the Title VII and X programs, the financing of land remains free of government insurance programs and the subsequent involvement in setting performance standards for credit and development. Partly because of this, a hodge-podge of sometimes expensive techniques are used to finance acquisition of undeveloped land. Periodic illiquidity, high interest rates, low loan–value ratios, extra charges and discounting, secured mortgages, and lump sum payments are more the rule than the exception.

We recommend that the federal government immediately initiate a short-term study of the impact of current land financing processes on the conversion process. This study should not only inventory the current practices, but also describe the effect of the practices on selecting participants in the conversion process, the cost of land, the nature and content of preservicing options, and local development patterns.

We hope that this study is directed at making definitive recommendations concerning the benefits and costs of possible development of a federal insurance program extending far beyond Title VII and X to cover most land acquisitions (consistent, perhaps, with local planning guidelines); federal support or participation in regulated privately initiated insurance efforts involving land acquisition; and development of a secondary mortgage market for land.

NOTES

1. Rodwin, L. *Nations and cities*. Boston: Houghton Mifflin Co., 1970. P. 3.
2. The Subcommittee reviewed most reports and papers on urban growth and land problems prepared by and for presidential, departmental, and legislative groups during the past 12 years. Many of these reports are listed in the bibliography attached to this paper.
3. The judgment of the Subcommittee concerning population is premised on trend line and time series analyses of the 1960–1970 U.S. Census.
4. High and low projections from U.S. Census, Series A and D, 1960.
5. Urban Research Group. *Preliminary draft of trends in growth*. Oak Ridge, Tennessee, 1971. Chapter I, p. 18. See also the discussion in Alonso, The mirage of new towns. *The Public Interest*, Spring 1970.
6. National Committee on Urban Growth Policy. *The new city*. New York: Praeger Publishers, 1969. P. 172.
7. *Op. cit.* Urban Research Group.
8. Milgram, G. *U.S. land prices—Directions and dynamics*. Research Report No. 13 for National Commission on Urban Problems. Washington, D.C.: U.S. Government Printing Office, 1968. P. 19.
9. *Ibid*.
10. President's Committee on Urban Housing. *A decent home*. Washington, D.C.: U.S. Government Printing Office, 1969. P. 141.
11. Schmidt, A. A. Suburban land appreciation. *Journal of the American Institute of Planners*, January 1970, 36, 39.
12. *Ibid*, P. 40.
13. Studies reviewed by the Subcommittee include S. Maisel, Background Information on costs of land for single family housing. *Report on housing*

47

in California–Appendix. (San Francisco: Governor's Advisory Commission on Housing Problems, April 1963); National Association of Home Builders, How land and lot costs went up in four years, *Special report* (Washington, D.C., 1965); A. A. Schmidt, *Converting land from rural to urban uses* (Washington, D.C.: Resources for the Future, 1968); F. G. Mittlebach, *Patterns of land utilization and costs: A study of Los Angeles* (Los Angeles: UCLA, 1967 Mimeo); G. Milgram, *The city expands* (Washington, D.C.: HUD, 1967.

14. Milgram, G. *Estimates of value of land in U.S.* Preliminary Report. New York: National Bureau of Economic Research, 1970. Table 5, p. 15.

15. Manvel, A. D. *Trends in value of real estate and land: 1956 to 1960.* Research Report No. 12. Washington, D.C.: National Commission on Urban Problems, 1968.

16. Land speculation is often seen as the cause and effect of all that is wrong with the urbanization process, perhaps understandably given the marginal state of our knowledge, but it is unfair given the apparent facts. The "speculator" is often loosely defined given the number of intermediaries and profit centers involved. Excess profits are not commonplace or widespread, as indicated in the text. Many analysts neglect to calculate the possible "benefits" of those playing speculative roles, particularly in the rationing of land and in the absorption of holding costs until land is ripe for development.

17. Milgram, G. *U.S. land prices–Directions and Dynamics.* Research Report No. 13 for National Commission on Urban Problems. Washington, D.C.: U.S. Government Printing Office, 1968. P. 35.

18. The farmer and the developer.

19. These observers include W. Alonso, *Location and land use: Toward a general theory of land rent* (Cambridge: Harvard University Press, 1964); W. R. Seyfried, The centrality of urban land values, *Land Economics*, August 1963, 39, 275-284. S. Czomonski, Effects of public investment on urban land values, *Journal of the American Institute of Planners*, July 1966, 32, 204-216. Also, see previously cited reports of Maisel, Mittlebach, and Milgram.

20. Clawson, M. *Suburban land conversion in the United States.* Baltimore, Maryland: John Hopkins Press, 1972. P. 123.

21. Data from Land Use Subcommittee discussions initiated with developers and state officials.

22. Milgram, G. *The city expands: A study of the conversion of land from rural to urban use–Philadelphia, 1945-62.* Philadelphia: University of Pennsylvania, Institute for Environmental Studies, 1967; S. Czomonski. Effects of public investments on urban land values. *Journal of the American Institute of Planners,* July 1966, 32, 204-216.

23. *Ibid.,* G. Milgram.

24. Kamm, S. *Land availability for housing and urban growth.* Washington, D.C.: House of Representatives, Committee on Banking and Currency, June 1971. P. 275.

25. New ideas in land planning—Cluster plan cuts his costs by one-third. *Journal of Homebuilding*, May 1962, 16, 76.
26. Comprehensive Planning Section of the Howard County Planning Commission. *Howard County, 1985*. Technical report. April 1967. P. 38a. All estimates based on 68,276 dwelling units in 1985, compared to 13,600 in 1965, or an increase of 54,676 in the 20-year period.
27. Table developed from data present in U.S. Department of Housing and Urban Development's *Annual Reports*, 1950-1970.
28. Kamm, S. *Land availability for housing and urban growth.* Washington, D.C.: House of Representatives, Committee on Banking and Currency, June 1971. P. 269.
29. Maisel, S. Background information on costs of land for single family housing. *Housing in California—Appendix*. San Francisco: Governor's Advisory Commission on Housing Problems, April 1963.
30. Several difficulties are inherent in demonstration programs, including (a) the political problem of limiting demonstrations to a predefined number of areas; (b) the evaluative problem of providing policy and program information within a reasonable time; and (c) the problem of choice in selecting areas that provide replicable experience. We feel that these problems can be overcome through careful design of each proposed demonstration and careful development of appropriate monitoring and evaluation programs.
31. Subcommittee observations based on a summary review of suburban budgets in select metropolitan areas.
32. Acquisition of land by political jurisdictions outside their boundaries.
33. If the costs of public services were immediately assessed to contiguous property, the impact on prices of raw land would be marginal. Obvious difficulties in determining the benefits for assessment purposes have yet to be resolved.
34. Public Law 91-609, 91st Congress, H.R. 19436, December 31, 1970, Title VII, Part B, Section D.
35. National Committee on Urban Growth Policy. *The new city.* New York: Praeger Publishers, 1969.
36. Subcommittee estimates of acreage needs.
37. Even so-called satellite communities or communities in fringe areas would require heavier burdens on low-income families than more affluent families due to the location of jobs.
38. "Most of the benefits resulting from extra costs . . . would be of the kind for which no direct revenues could be collected . . . the private sector—including the beneficiaries themselves—will not voluntarily pay the extra costs of producing these benefits; therefore, the government would have to incur much larger expenditures for urban growth in new cities than in other forms."
A. Downs, Alternative forms of future urban growth, *Journal of the American Institute of Planners*, January 1970, 36, 6.
39. Rapkin, C. *The private insurance of home mortgages.* Philadelphia: University of Pennsylvania, 1967. P. 1.

SELECTED BIBLIOGRAPHY

Alonso, W. The mirage of new towns. *The Public Interest*, Spring 1970.

Alonso, W. *Location and land use: Toward a general theory of land rent.* Cambridge: Harvard University Press, 1964.

Burns, L., & Mittlebach, F. G. Location—Fourth determinant of residential value. *Appraisal Journal*, April 1964, 32.

Colorado Department of Highways Land Economic Study. *Interstate 25, North of Denver*. Denver, 1962.

Czomonski, S. Effects of public investment on urban land values. *Journal of The American Institute of Planners*, July 1966, 32, 204–216.

Eichler, E., & Kaplan, M. *The community builders*. Berkeley: University of California Press, 1967.

Downs, A. Alternative forms of future growth in U.S. *Journal of The American Institute of Planners*, January 1970, 36, 3–11.

Gaffney, M., & Mutz, R. *Land as an element of housing costs: The effects of public policies and practices: The effects of housing development.* Report No. S-324. Arlington, Virginia: Institute for Defense Analyses, 1968.

Goldsmith, R. W. *The national wealth of U.S. in postwar world.* Princeton: Princeton University Press, 1962.

Haig, R. M. *Major economic factors in metropolitan growth and arrangement.* Vol. 1. New York: Regional Survey of New York and Its Environs, 1927.

Kaplan, M. The role of the planner and developer in the new community. *Washington University Law Library*, February 1965, 1965, 88–104

Kenduch, J. W. The wealth of United States. *Finance*, January 1967, 85, 10–13, 34.

Maisel, S. D. Background information on costs of land for single-family housing. *Housing in California—Appendix*. San Francisco: Governor's Advisory Commission on Housing Problems, April 1963.

Manvel, A. D. *Trends in value of real estate and land: 1956 to 1966.* Research Report No. 12. Washington, D.C.: National Commission on Urban Problems, 1968.

Milgram, G. *Estimates of value of land in U.S.–1952–1968.* Preliminary Report. New York: National Bureau of Economic Research, 1970.

Milgram, G. *The city expands: A study of the conversion of land from rural to urban use–Philadelphia, 1945–62.* Philadelphia: University of Pennsylvania, Institute for Environmental Studies, 1967.

Milgram, G. *U.S. land prices–Directions and Dynamics.* Research Report No. 13 for National Commission on Urban Problems. Washington, D.C.: U.S. Government Printing Office, 1968.

Mittlebach, F. G. Residential land values in Los Angeles County. *Housing in California–Appendix.* San Francisco: Governor's Advisory Commission on Housing Problems, April 1963.

Mittlebach, F. G. *Patterns of land utilization and costs: A study of Los Angeles.* Los Angeles: University of California, Graduate School of Business Administration, 1967. (mimeographed)

National Association of Homebuilders. How land and lot costs went up in four years. Special Report 65-8. Washington, D.C.: National Association of Homebuilders, 1965.

Neutze, G. M. *The use of land and the suburban apartment boom.* Washington, D.C.: Resources for the Future, 1966.

Pendleton, W. C. Relation of highway accessibility to urban real estate values. *The Highway Research Record,* No. 16, 1963.

Real Estate Research Corporation. *The influence of highway improvements on land use patterns.* Chicago, 1958.

Schmidt, A. A. Suburban land appreciation. *Journal of the American Institute of Planners,* January 1970, 36, 38–43.

Urban Research Group. *Preliminary draft of trends in growth.* Oak Ridge National Labs, December 1971.

URBAN GROWTH REPORTS
REVIEWED BY THE
SUBCOMMITTEE

The Subcommittee studied several legislative, presidential, and administration task force reports concerned with urban growth problems. They included, but were not limited to, the following:

1. The President's Task Force on Suburban Problems. *Final report* (the "Haar report"). Prepared under C. M. Haar, Assistant Secretary for Metropolitan Development. Washington, D.C.: U.S. Department of Housing and Urban Development, 1968.
2. U.S. Congress, Joint Economic Committee, Subcommittee on Urban Affairs. *Urban America: Goals and problems.* 90th Cong., 1st Sess. Washington, D.C.: U.S. Government Printing Office, 1967.
3. Report and Background Papers of the President's Committee on Urban Housing, 1968 (Kaiser Commission).
4. U.S. Department of Agriculture. *National growth and distribution.* Washington, D.C.: U.S. Government Printing Office, 1968.
5. National Committee on Urban Growth Policy. *The new city.* New York: Praeger, 1969.
6. The Task Force on Planning Requirements (Interdepartmental). *A unified planning requirements system: Recommendations to improve the management and effectiveness of federal planning requirements.* Washington, D.C.: U.S. Department of Housing and Urban Development, December 1969.
7. The Task Force on Planning Assistance (Interdepartmental). *A federal planning assistance strategy: Recommendations to improve the management and effectiveness of federal planning assistance programs.* Washington, D.C.: U.S. Department of Housing and Urban Development, October 1969.
8. Subcommittee on Housing and Urban Affairs of the Committee on Banking

and Currency, United States Senate. Hearings on *Housing and urban development legislation of 1970.* 91st Cong., 2nd Sess., Parts 1 and 2.

9. National Goals Research Staff. *Toward balanced growth: Quantity with quality.* Washington, D.C.: U.S. Government Printing Office, 1970.

10. Hearings before the *Ad Hoc* Subcommittee on Urban Growth of the Committee on Banking and Currency, House of Representatives, 91st Cong., 2nd Sess., Parts I, II, and III. 1970.

11. Senate Report 91-1435 on *The National Land Use Policy Act of 1970.* S-3354 amending the Water Resources Planning Act of 1965.

12. Paper submitted to Subcommittee on Housing Panels, Committee on Banking and Currency, House of Representatives, 92nd Cong., June 1971.

13. Report and Background Papers of the National Commission on Urban Problems to the Congress and to the President of the United States, 1968 (Douglas Commission).

14. Domestic Council, Executive Office of the President. *The President's 1971 environmental program: Toward more rational use of the land.* Book 2. Washington, D.C.: U.S. Government Printing Office, 1971.

15. Public Land Law Review Commission.

16. Assistant Secretary Jackson's 1970 and 1971 Task Forces on Urban Growth Problems. Unpublished draft reports. Washington, D.C.: U.S. Department of Housing and Urban Development.

17. President of the United States to the Congress of the United States. Reports on national housing goals. 1969, 1970, 1971.

Date Due